you feel
good
about

Finding a job you feel good about

by

Clifford B. Garrison, Ed.D.
William J. McCurdy, S.J.
Paul J. Munson, Ed.D.
Patricia Pavlik
Jean D. Saunders
Kathryn Sims
Dorothea Telis

Argus Communications
Niles, Illinois

Design by Gene Tarpey and Collin Fry

FIRST EDITION

© Copyright Argus Communication 1977
All rights reserved. No portion of this book may be
reproduced, stored in a retrieval system, or transmitted
in any form by any means—electronic, mechanical,
photocopying, recording, or otherwise—without prior
permission of the copyright owner.

Printed in the United States of America.

Argus Communications
7440 Natchez Avenue
Niles, Illinois 60648

International Standard Book Number 0-913592-88-9
Library of Congress Number 77-80189

3 4 5 6 7 8 9 0

Acknowledgment

The authors are responsible for the creation, research, revision, and field test of the Career Motivation Project. Out of that experience has come much of the material in this book. The Career Motivation Project was originally funded by the United States Office of Education, ESEA, Title III; New York State Education Department, Bureau of Guidance; and the Union Free School District, East Aurora, New York.

We are also grateful to the numerous co-workers and friends whose kind helpfulness aided so much in the development of this material.

Contents

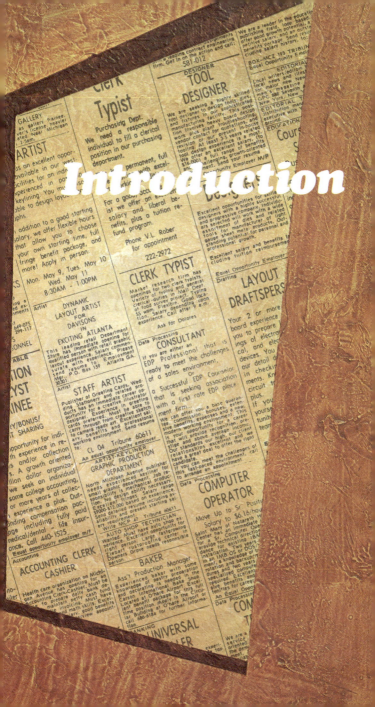

Introduction

THE BIG DECISION

Sometimes . . . . . I'm confused!

How will I know how to choose a job?

Will I like the job I choose?

Will it make me happy?

I want a change, but to what?

In other words, will I fit into future worlds?

These questions continually face students and their elders alike—"Which job, which career, promises me fulfillment? Dare I change jobs or career plans in the hopes of finding a truly satisfying place in the work world?"

This book will not choose a career for you; it won't even tell you how to get a different job.

Rather, it is a step-by-step process of helping discover a future profession or a new job or profession.

This is a guided, do-it-yourself way of finding out the types of work that will be most fulfilling to your personality.

To do it, you must find the facts about your character, about your personality.

Career choices will be most satisfying when they are compatible with our own character traits.

These include:

- **Successes,** tasks we do or have done well,
- **Strengths,** outstanding character traits,
- **Career values,** the job conditions we require,
- **Interests,** things that catch and hold our attention,
- **Abilities,** things we do well or very well.

Specific job choices will always be yours alone. But first you need to know why certain work satisfies you and why other jobs are barely tolerable.

Schools and libraries overflow with career information. But none of it has the personal touch. None tells exactly where your special personality fits. Each of the following pages concentrates on you—your successes, strengths, abilities, interests, and career values.

The final Full Picture Chart and Job Skill Chart enable you to line up your special interests and abilities with definite *job/career possibilities.*

Work: What Is It?

It certainly is something that we do or talk about nearly every day. If we looked it up in the dictionary, we would probably come up with a definition something like this: mental or physical effort used to do or perform a task to achieve a goal or result; the labor or duty from which one earns his or her living.

But if we think about it a bit, work is much more than that. How many different definitions could we make up to fit the kinds of things we say about work all the time!

We talk of an artist's *work*.

A neighbor has *work* to do at home.

Someone brings *work* home from the office.

The weekend hobbyist is going to *work* on a stamp collection.

We promise someone that we'll *work* on an idea.

Friends have a problem that they are *working* out.

A young boy says his parents are at *work*.

All these different activities are covered by that little word *work*. It means jobs, careers, hobbies, sports, even the ways we create and maintain our living conditions. That is why people in government and education concerned with career preparation view work in very different terms from the way they did only a few years ago. They now recognize that for a person's lifework to be satisfying, it must include all of these elements:

- a wage or salary that provides a secure economic base,
- agreeable working conditions (whether outdoors on a steel girder or inside in a comfortable chair),
- fulfilling hobbies or recreational life,
- a "well done" feeling that contributes to good family and social relations.

If you now have a job or are aiming toward a job that does not really fulfill these conditions, you are going to experience a good deal of unhappiness. If you want to get out of or avoid that situation, we hope this book will help you.

Dead End

What a terrible ring those words have!

Yet, too many of us end up there. Have you ever told yourself, "My life just doesn't seem to be satisfying," and then asked, "Is there something wrong with me?"

Chances are that there is nothing wrong with you, for dissatisfaction in itself is not wrong. It is when we don't do anything about it that we foul up our lives. Dissatisfaction should trigger action, not frustration. It simply tells us that we need to take some steps to discover our own needs and then act to meet them. This can be a very simple or a very complicated process. What we are proposing here is not that complicated or difficult.

Let's start by asking if you are dissatisfied with your

- job or career?
- hobbies, recreational, or social life?
- living condition?

Then let's look at some typical situations. Perhaps you will find yourself there.

WHITE-COLLAR WORKER

You're punching a calculator, shuffling papers and figures all day, dreading every minute. Your co-worker at the next desk seems happy as a lark. But you wish you could walk out of the place and never come back.

YOU'RE RETIRED

Your work—your job—was your whole life. You never prepared to have nothing to do. Your work took so much time that you never developed hobbies or traveled. Your wife is always busy with something that interests her. You have the constant feeling that you ought to go to the office. But you can't!

HIGH SCHOOL SENIOR

"Are there any right career decisions?" There are two or three directions you could see yourself going. They seem equally interesting. But which will be the most satisfying?

OVEREDUCATED

You really enjoyed every minute of your education. You have no regrets, except that the job market has no crying need for your degrees right now. Who can help you decide which of your skills *are* needed today?

MOTHER OF YOUNG CHILDREN

Nobody ever told you that you would feel trapped. You love your children, but twenty-four hours a day with them only makes you wonder if you can be anything but a mother. You don't want to give up your family. You just want to spend an hour or two a day doing something else.

ART STUDENT

Art, that's where your future lies. Designing interests you. But what? Clothes, cars, book covers? You're having trouble deciding on the type of work world that will make you feel comfortable and accepted.

HIGH SCHOOL SOPHOMORE

You've been working for your father, repairing transmissions. But you're all thumbs; it's really not your thing. They say you have the brains to go to college, but that doesn't exactly turn you on either. Your counselors, your parents, all think that you should make some decisions.

EMPTY NESTER

Suddenly, life has no meaning. Your youngest child just got a job and moved into her own apartment. You're lost. You need to get out of the house and find something to fill up your time—not necessarily a job, but at least something that would make you feel useful and needed again.

BOUND FOR THE TRADES

Your father is a tradesman. You admire him, want to follow him. But being an electrician holds no interest for you. Where else would you fit?

16

JUST OUT OF HIGH SCHOOL

You think you'll go to work someday. But for now you just want to drift, see things, and make enough to keep you going. Your family is in medicine, law, you name it. But it seems to you that there are other values. Money is the name of their game, but maybe it's not yours.

TROUBLED EXECUTIVE

The corporate life can get to a person. Job security? The question is always there. So you've decided to make a change. The problem now is, what kind of change? You have never given much thought to what else you can do.

UNSKILLED LABORER

You took this job because you had no idea of what else you could do. Your family has to eat. Hard work never bothered you. You're just confused about which type of hard work would really make you feel best.

WANTS A FAMILY

Married life is definitely for you, with no outside career until your children are gone. But you would like to work for a few years anyway, at least until marriage. And you want to be happy with the work you do after graduation, even if only for a short time.

ATHLETE

You are assured of college scholarships. But you don't want to waste the time and money studying a field that's not going to be useful after your athletic days are over. What if you choose to stay in sports? Can you earn money in some aspect of it besides competition?

HIGH SCHOOL SOPHOMORE

Business definitely interests you. Your job as clerk in a local clothing store makes you think that you would like to continue in the business after graduation. You are not sure about college; can you go as far as you intend to go without it?

NOT ENOUGH EDUCATION

You quit school, couldn't decide on a career. Now you're sorry, but you still don't know what to do. You're just moving from job to job, hoping to fall into something that suits you. After all, you tell yourself, you have lots of time to find something you really like. Actually, you're just drifting and not very happy about it.

HONOR STUDENT

They say that with your grades, many career possibilities are open. So, your hard work is paying off. Your science courses have been the most rewarding. But science careers can take many directions. Should you teach, do research? You just don't know.

OUT OF WORK

Your company has just gone out of business. There is no choice; you must find a new job. You've been considering another line of work for some time. Here's your chance to give it a try. But do you dare risk the chance of not being satisfied there? You wish there were a way to know.

COLLEGE BOUND

More education, that's your goal. Why?—because the entire atmosphere appeals to you. You want the experience. But you're undecided about an exact career direction. You have several ideas but have made no concrete decisions. Who can help you?

Did any of these situations strike home? Do you share some of these feelings? If you do, then it's time to do something about it.

My
Good Times

HOW DO YOU FIND WORK THAT MAKES YOU HAPPY?

How do you find work that makes you feel happy, comfortable, and successful—a job in which all of the ingredients add up to give you a satisfied feeling by the end of each day?

Can't be! Or can it be? You sure hope so!

Being happy with our work has a different meaning for each of us. Some of us want money and fame; others want short hours, peace, and privacy. No matter. If we have what fits us, we can be happy.

Another way to say it is that if our values and our life-styles coincide, then we probably have a satisfied feeling. VALUES? Values simply refer to "the things which are most important to us," the inner signposts that guide our lives.

There are as many sets of values as there are people on earth. We each have our own value system. The following combinations probably characterize somebody, maybe you. Perhaps you look for these kinds of satisfactions in a job:

- helping others
- working on a team
- being respected

- making lots of money
- achieving
- gaining prestige

- having willpower
- exercising leadership
- creating order

Can't find yourself here?

Don't be concerned if these combinations describe people other than yourself. This book is designed to help you discover *your* values.

A Personal Value System

What really makes up your life-style?

Answering this question is not quite as complicated or as difficult as it may seem. The step-by-step process described on the following pages produces a chart that helps you find out about your own values.

But does this have anything to do with finding suitable work? It definitely does. The suitability of your work depends upon a good correlation between your values, abilities, and interests. They have a great deal to do with each other.

Good Times Chart: Step One

Filling out a chart is a mechanical process, but you will want to think through your answers before marking your Good Times Chart. The first step is very important for completing the chart in a way that will be useful for you.

Relax. Try to recall satisfying, successful experiences *at any time in your life* from birth right up to the present.

My Good Times Char

I . . .

1. was able to make new things, find new solutions, be creative.

2. gained new information, used insight and judgment.

3. established or strengthened positive relationships by working closely with others.

4. did something I was sure I could do.

5. gained respect from others because of the importance of what I did.

6. was able to plan or organize in an orderly manner.

7. got others to follow my lead or directions.

8. did what I wanted, my way, made my own decisions.

9. added to the beauty of my world.

10. was free to be the kind of person I want to be.

11. fully used my talents and energy to do my best.

12. helped others physically and emotionally.

13. obtained a good income for my accomplishment.

14. worked under the direction or guidance of people I admired.

15. did a variety of new and different things.

16. kept at things until the job was done.

17. worked with printed matter in evaluating or interpreting information.

18. met or worked with people.

19. used my hands or physical ability.

AT HOME	AT WORK OR SCHOOL	FREE TIME	SPECIAL MOMENT	FANTASY	TOTALS
	major office	Olympic mts			

HAPPY OR SATISFYING EXPERIENCES
—at home
—at work or school
—during free time (away from work or school)
—in a special moment of happiness or success

Take time to think. Even very pleasant memories come back slowly sometimes.

Below are four examples of the kinds of happy experiences one might think of for the Good Times Chart.

AT HOME

As a child, Jennie had long hair. But her mother's favorite job was *not* washing hair. When Jennie was about eight years old, she decided to try doing the job herself. She tried and succeeded. She was happy, and so was her mother.

AT SCHOOL

Bob's grade school met in the same building as the high school. The schools shared teachers. Bob liked English composition. In eighth grade, whenever he finished assignments early, his teacher let him work on one of the high school club newspapers. It made him feel proud.

FREE TIME

Carl's older brother and his friends let Carl join in most of their games, even though he was two years younger. It made him feel very grown-up.

SPECIAL MOMENT

Sharon moved to another city. After a month she was hired for a job she had really wanted, but had been too shy to apply for at first.

To get started, list experiences that made you feel good, happy, proud, and/or successful. Don't worry if time periods overlap.

At home _____

_____

At school or work_____

_____

Free time (away from school or work)_____

_____

Special moment (of happiness or success) __

_____

4th July

Jack

8,000

You're going to use these experiences to fill in your Good Times Chart on pages 26–27. To do that, you'll have to sum them up in a word or two and write them in the space just below the headings: At Home, At School or Work, and so on.

For example, if you had picked experiences like the ones above, your Good Times Chart would start like this:

AT HOME	AT WORK OR SCHOOL	FREE TIME	SPECIAL MOMENT	
hair	*news work*	*games*	*got job*	

Just list those four experiences right now. The "Fantasy" square comes later.

Now look at the Reward List at the left-hand side of your Good Times Chart. Rewards are reasons:

why our experiences made us feel good, happy, or successful.

why we remember those experiences with pride and pleasure.

Read through the list and think about those rewards. Then go down the column under each of the experiences you listed. Wherever

31

the reward seems to give you a reason why your experience made you feel good, make a check in the box on that line. For example, if Jennie were filling out the chart, she might check off her chart for the hair-washing experience like this:

My Good Times Chart

I . . .	AT HOME *hair*	AT WORK OR SCHOOL *new work*
1. was able to make new things, find new solutions, be creative.	✓	
2. gained new information, used insight and judgment.		
3. established or strengthened positive relationships by working closely with others.		
4. did something I was sure I could do.	✓	
5. gained respect from others because of the importance of what I did.	✓	

Each check represents a satisfaction, whether slight, medium, or great.

So be sure to check even the slightest reasons.

Good Times Chart: Step Two

Now you are ready for the second stage of the sorting process. Go over the Reward List again *for each experience* and circle the rewards already checked representing medium or great satisfaction. This is a process of separating the smaller kinds of satisfactions from the ones which brought you a greater feeling of fulfillment. Be selective. For example, if Jennie were doing it for her hair-washing experience, that first column might look like this:

32

My Good Times Chart

I . . .	AT HOME hair	AT WORK OR SCHOOL new work
1. was able to make new things, find new solutions, be creative.	✔	
2. gained new information, used insight and judgment.		
3. established or strengthened positive relationships by working closely with others.		
4. did something I was sure I could do.	✔ (circled)	
5. gained respect from others because of the importance of what I did.	✔ (circled)	

Now refer again to the full Good Times Chart on pages 26–27. Go through the Reward List one more time for each experience. Using a colored felt-tip pen or colored pencil, shade in the already checked and circled squares that represent your very highest personal satisfactions.

Remember, these should be the rewards that brought you the deepest and most important kinds of fulfillment, not just surface enjoyment.

If Jennie were doing it, her chart for the hair-washing experience would look like this:

My Good Times Chart

I . . .	AT HOME hair	AT WORK OR SCHOOL new work
1. was able to make new things, find new solutions, be creative.	✔	
2. gained new information, used insight and judgment.		
3. established or strengthened positive relationships by working closely with others.		
4. did something I was sure I could do.	✔ (circled)	
5. gained respect from others because of the importance of what I did.	✔ (circled)	

FANTASY JOB

There is still another step to filling out your Good Times Chart. When you finish it you will be ready to make some discoveries about your values—the motivations that shape your life-style.

You have probably noticed the column labeled "Fantasy" at the upper right of your chart and have wondered what it is all about. It refers to a fantasy, or ideal, job.

Imagine the kind of work you would *like* to be doing five years from now. Just let your imagination run wild.

> Where would you live?
> How would you live?
> What kind of salary would you be getting?

What other rewards (fun, excitement, prestige, respect, security, etc.) would you get?

In imagining your fantasy job, assume that you have all the ability and training you would need. Perhaps the job you want does not even exist today, but you can dream about it.

To give you an idea of the kind of thing we mean, one of the authors of this book dreamed up her own fantasy job. She has always enjoyed editing books, but she lives in a large northern metropolitan area where the cold winters and constant hustle and bustle sometimes get her down. So she imagined a fantasy job like this:

She would edit books, but while living on a South Sea island. Her salary would only have to be enough to keep her comfortable and allow for an occasional trip back to the mainland to visit friends and family. Her main rewards would be doing work she likes and enjoying a peaceful and beautiful environment.

Now think about *your own* fantasy job. Describe it to yourself in some detail. Then take two or three words that sum it up and write them in the space under "Fantasy" the way you did for the experiences in the first four columns on the Good Times Chart.

Do the sorting process as before:

Check ✓ off any reward, whether slight, medium, or great.

Circle ⊘ already checked rewards which represent medium or great satisfaction.

Color in ✓ already circled rewards that brought you deep, personal satisfaction.

What Can Your Good Times Chart Tell You?

It is finally time to find out what the chart is all about. Here is how to do it.

First assign a numerical value to each reward. Score as follows:

a check only ✓ = 1

a check and a circle ⊘ = 3

a shaded square ✓ = 5

Then total up the score for each reward by adding across and write the total in the column at the far right of the chart.

We now need to provide some *key words* or *values* that will finally put the Good Times Chart all together to make sense for you.

Each reward indicates a value, or something which may be very important to you. For example, the first reward says:

"was able to make new things, to find new solutions, be creative."

This relates to "creativity," or the fact that you must be creating in some way in order to feel really happy.

Matching the key words or values to the
rewards on the chart, we discover that:

was able to make new things,
find new solutions, be creative.

corresponds to creativity

gained new information, used
insight and judgment.

corresponds to knowledge

established or strengthened
positive relationships by
working closely with others.

corresponds to relating

did something I was sure I could
do.

corresponds to security

gained respect from others
because of the importance of
what I did.

corresponds to prestige

was able to plan or organize in
an orderly manner.

corresponds to order

got others to follow my lead or
directions.

corresponds to leadership

did what I wanted, my way,
made my own decisions.

corresponds to independence

added to the beauty of my
world.

corresponds to beauty

was free to be the kind of
person I want to be.

>*corresponds to self-realization*

fully used my talents and energy
to do my best.

>*corresponds to achievement*

helped others physically or
emotionally.

>*corresponds to social service*

obtained a good income for my
accomplishment.

>*corresponds to economic reward*

worked under the direction or
guidance of people I admired.

>*corresponds to cooperation*

did a variety of new and
different things.

>*corresponds to variety*

kept at things until the job was
done.

>*corresponds to endurance*

worked with printed matter in
evaluating or interpreting
information.

>*corresponds to data*

met or worked with people.

>*corresponds to people*

used my hands or physical
ability.

>*corresponds to things*

Now look back at the totals column of your Good Times Chart. Check the five rewards that you gave the highest scores to. Which values do those rewards correspond to? The answer tells you what your top values are—the ideals that guide your daily life. It is most helpful to see them written down, to see exactly what moves you to live as you do.

List your top values below.

_____

_____

_____

_____

_____

INDUSTRIOUS
DEDICATED
OUTGOING
TALENTED
STABLE
GO-GETTER
TIRELESS
FLEXIBLE
ACCURATE
EAGER
WITTY
NEAT
TACTFUL
GENTLE
CURIOUS

My Strengths

WINNING STRENGTHS

Satisfying work rests on several foundation blocks:
Values Strengths Abilities Interests

The Good Times Chart has helped you to discover much about your values. We turn now to the second building block:
STRENGTHS.

We all have strengths, numerous and differing characteristics that help us "shine" in one way or another. Taken together, our strong points make us more suited for some kinds of work than for others.

One person may be
—a thinker
—an organizer
—a methodical worker.

These may be the characteristics of a strong executive type. Someone else may show obvious signs of
—warmth
—empathy
—cooperation
—dependability.

Persons with these strong points might find their greatest happiness in social service or working very closely with people.

No matter, everybody is different; everybody is a valuable person because he or she is different from everybody else.

What about your strong points? What characteristics make you strong and unique?

Perhaps it is difficult for some of us to evaluate our own character, especially if in our childhood we were told that "it's not right to brag" or that we "never do anything right."

For this process, try to be objective. That is, mentally step outside of your body, walk several feet away, and watch yourself as if you were trailing a good friend. Watch for the things you do well—being kind, perhaps, or organizing and keeping things running well.

Think. Think of the good things about yourself. On the next two pages there is a list to help you focus your thinking. Study it carefully for strengths that describe you. Study the entire list for a while before you start.

Put a check ✔ beside each word or phrase that describes you, whether you think you are that way all the time or just part of the time.

STRENGTH WORD LIST

13 busy
3 kind
9 artistic
4 careful
13 convincing
3 friendly
9 musical
4 steady
13 energetic
3 trusting
9 gentle
4 loyal
13 go-getter
3 understanding
9 charming
4 stable
5 distinctive
11 perfectionist
8 self-determining
16 pursuing
5 dignified
11 ambitious
8 individualistic
16 steadfast
5 poised
11 competent
8 strong-willed
16 motivated
5 admirable

5 sharp
11 capable
8 certain
16 overcoming
5 looked up to
11 dedicated
8 courageous
16 consistent
5 honorable
11 productive
8 independent
16 determined
5 respected
11 efficient
8 confident
16 tireless
13 industrious
3 thoughtful
9 expressive
4 settled
13 persuasive
3 affectionate
9 graceful
4 deliberate
13 influential
3 accepting
9 attractive
4 cautious
13 competitive

44

11	disciplined	3	giving
8	self-reliant	9	appreciative
16	persistent	4	reliable
6	neat	7	leader
12	caring	14	eager
2	aware	10	growing
1	full of ideas	15	active
6	accurate	7	planner
12	helpful	14	unselfish
2	thinker	10	self-aware
1	clever	15	likes new ideas
6	exact	7	manager
12	humorous	14	cooperative
2	well-informed	10	self-directed
1	creative	15	open-minded
6	orderly	7	forceful
12	outgoing	14	dependable
2	searching	10	adjusted
1	original	15	adaptable
7	fair-minded	6	systematic
14	considerate	12	encouraging
10	fulfilled	2	curious
15	flexible	1	unique
7	organizer	6	precise
14	tactful	12	trustworthy
10	committed	2	knowledgeable
15	spontaneous	1	imaginative
7	commanding	6	practical
14	tolerant	12	sociable
10	goal-directed	2	intelligent
15	progressive	1	witty
7	analytical	6	predictable
14	faithful	12	comforting
10	authentic	2	inquiring
15	adventurous	1	talented

Often friends can be more objective and see your good points more easily than you can. So if you have the opportunity, share the Strength Word List with a friend or two. Ask them to pick out and check the strengths they see in you. They can both confirm your feelings and bring out qualities that you might miss.

After both you and your friends have identified your strengths by checking the words that describe you, you are ready to develop your strength profile. Begin by making a list of all the words that were checked. In making the list be sure to include both the words you checked and the ones your friends checked, and in each case also list the number that appears with the word or phrase. For example, the beginning of a list might look like this:

13 busy
3 kind
3 trusting
9 charming

Got your whole list done? Chances are you never really thought much about some of those strengths before. But they are really yours. Were there some that both you and your friends picked? Are they some of your strongest points?

Go over the list carefully. Think about those strengths for a while. Then pick out the ten you think are your chief strengths. Write these in a second list beside the first. Don't forget to write each word's number right alongside.

The broad picture of your character strengths should be becoming clear. You have chosen some. Your friends have probably confirmed them and maybe they have suggested others you would not have thought about.

Now you are ready for a final profiling of your strengths. Go back over the whole list—not just the ten chief strengths—and pick five that give the best picture of the strong you. You see, you might want to use one of the lesser, but important, strengths to round out the picture of yourself. You might, for example, not feel that being *well-informed* is one of your greatest strengths, but adding it to the other four you have picked brings the description closer to the way you see yourself.

Write your five profile strengths in a third list beside the other two, remembering again to write each word's code number alongside. Now using those numbers, you can convert the descriptive words into general strength categories.

1 = creativity
2 = knowledge
3 = relating
4 = security
5 = prestige
6 = order
7 = leadership
8 = independence
9 = beauty
10 = self-realization
11 = achievement
12 = social service
13 = economic reward
14 = cooperation
15 = variety
16 = endurance

Write your strength categories in the spaces provided below.

Little by little, you are learning what makes you tick.

Your strong character traits are:

_____

_____

_____

_____

_____

Save this list: you will need it later to finish your self-portrait.

DATA PEOPLE THINGS

Data,
People,
Things

WHAT DO YOU REALLY LIKE?

Deep inside, you feel your strong points. But you remain dissatisfied. Could it be that your work and your recreation are based on what *someone else thinks you ought to like to do?*

You know your own values, know that you have unused abilities and would like to explore them. Still, at times you find yourself doing what someone else thinks is right.

Here's a situation that describes what happened to one of the authors. It is the kind of thing that happens to too many of us.

Aptitude tests said that I should be a librarian. I didn't want to be a librarian. People told me to go to graduate school. I really wanted to work. But, like everyone else, I've done too many things that other people chose for me.

So, if you think that you can only dream about a job, only have fantasies about another way of life, put on a different thinking cap. Part of that dreaming can include a little exploration—sorting out your likes and dislikes—pinpointing the activities that stir your interest and fulfill you, instead of being just plain dull.

There are many different ways to classify the activities that interest people. The government likes to do it by dividing our interests into three general categories.

They're called:

- data
- people
- things

They may sound a little strange, but they are not all that complicated after they have been decoded.

Data

Some people find life most satisfying when they work or have hobbies that deal with the abstract. The accountant and the astronomer compile figures. The hobbyist stock-market investor and the serious cardplayer enjoy calculating odds. Each one likes a data task. It doesn't mean a dislike for people. It's just that these people have fun with abstract thought processes.

On the next page there is a list of DATA tasks—things to do involving numbers and words. Go over the list, and pick the two items that best represent your real interests. Rate them first and second, according to preference. Number 1 should be the task about which you get the feeling "I really enjoy doing that!" Put the numbers 1 and 2 next to your choices.

You may think that you are people-oriented; so at first you may not feel like choosing DATA tasks. But when you go through the list carefully, you may discover that there really is something there that you enjoy or can do well.

So run through the list and rate your DATA tasks. Read both the key words and definitions to get a clear picture before deciding.

DATA

_____
Combining, or synthesizing

Determine facts and bring information together to develop new knowledge.

_____
Arranging, or coordinating

Arrange and organize the time, place, and order of an activity.

_____
Figuring out, or analyzing

Evaluate and analyze information to figure out your course of action.

_____
Gathering, or compiling

Gather and sort information about people, numbers, or things.

_____
Computing

Use mathematics to solve problems involving numbers and quantities.

_____
Comparing

Use observed information or quantities to identify similarities or differences.

People

Some individuals must have continuous human contact. They thrive by always being in touch with another person. Their interests and values lie in people. Let's find out how

you rank tasks involving people. Go through
the list on the next page and again indicate
your first and second choices in the space
provided.

PEOPLE

_____ Counseling	Help people understand their values and clarify their goals.
_____ Peacemaking, or negotiating	Help groups or individuals make rules and decisions and solve problems.
_____ Teaching, or instructing	Help people gain skills and knowledge.
_____ Leading, or supervising	Motivate others, administer and oversee their work.
_____ Performing, or entertaining	Amuse or entertain others.
_____ Convincing, or persuading	Get others to do something or buy something.
_____ Speaking, and/or guiding	Provide people with information or directions.
_____ Serving	Work for, or help, others.

Things

We identify most hobbyists by the THINGS they make, produce, or collect. Anyone finding pleasure in Things likes to

—put them together
—take them apart
—collect them
—stock them
—alter them
—find them
—manipulate them.

For "things-oriented" people, an object has value above and beyond the use for which it was invented. For example, the mailman or the doctor uses a truck or car simply to get around town, as transportation. For the car buff, however, these vehicles become more important as objects to collect or work on than as transportation.

Rate your first and second preferences from the Things list on the next page.

THINGS

_____ Setting up	Install, adjust, or repair machines.
_____ Precision working	Work with machines that need very exact, careful operation.
_____ Skilled handling, manipulating	Use hands or tools to work, move, guide, or place objects.
_____ Feeding, off bearing	Guide, dump, or load things into, or remove from, machines and equipment.
_____ Handling	Use your hands and tools to move, carry, pack, or load things.
_____ Control, operate	Start, stop, control, or adjust the operation of stationary equipment and machinery involving use of gauges, valves, dials, switches, etc.
_____ Driving, operating	Start, stop, and control operation of mobile machines such as cranes, tractors, excavators, trucks, or buses.

Now look back at each list:

DATA

PEOPLE

THINGS

Think about the tasks marked. Choose the three you favor the most of all. (You may favor your second choice in one category over your first choice in another category.) Write your answers below.

Your Top Choices

_____

_____

_____

You've just had an opportunity to think about different kinds of work and how they involve data, people, or things. Are you beginning to get a clearer idea of the type of work you feel most comfortable with?

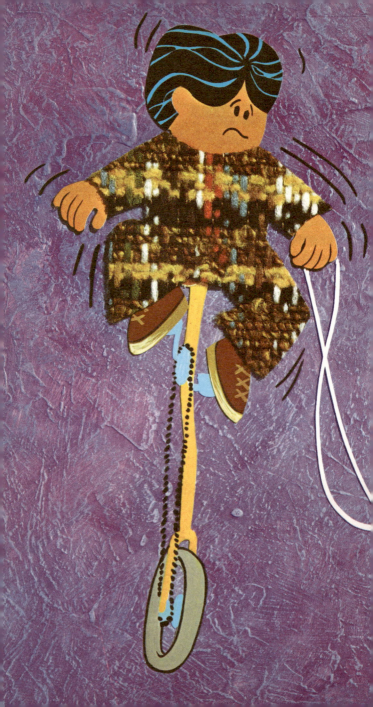

Abilities and Interests

WHAT DO YOU DO WELL AND WHAT DO YOU LIKE TO DO?

With data, people, and things you began to explore the general areas of your abilities and interests. Now here's your chance to get specific and rate yourself on two counts:

- ABILITY, or how well you *can* do something;
- INTEREST, or how much you *like* doing that thing.

For your own happiness, it is very important to have a clear picture of the things you want and like to do. For example: You might enjoy counseling even though you have no professional training for that activity. But you may have had a little practical experience. Now get specific. Is group counseling your thing? Perhaps not—you like to help just one person try to solve his or her problems.

Let's say there is another task for which you've had lots of training—photography. And within the general category of photography, you prefer to do nature photography.

You can . . .

Continuing the process of trying to discover your ideal vocation or avocation, you will rate your ability at quite specific things.

Each of us is aware of those things we do easily, with skill; conversely, we know about the difficult, unpleasant things we have to do.

On the following list, rate yourself according to ABILITY only, disregarding your likes and dislikes for the moment. Consider how well you *can do* these tasks, not how much you like or dislike them. Rate each task on a scale of 1 to 5:

1 means low or: "I have little or no ability."

5 means high or: "I have very great ability."

Numbers 2, 3, and 4 are degrees in between.

Rate yourself by circling the number that best indicates the amount of your ABILITY.

Abilities	*Your Rating*
Singing, playing, or reading music	1 2 3 4 5 *musical skill*
Leading or supervising others	1 2 3 4 5 *supervisory skill*
Communicating ideas to others	1 2 3 4 5 *communication skill*
Visualizing shapes and surfaces from seeing drawings or plans	1 2 3 4 5 *spatial relations skill*
Thinking through complicated problems, carrying out logical processes in the mind	1 2 3 4 5 *abstract reasoning skill*
Bringing together things, information, and/or people to accomplish a task	1 2 3 4 5 *organizational skill*
Helping others make decisions and solve their problems	1 2 3 4 5 *counseling skill*
Teaching a skill or passing on knowledge to others	1 2 3 4 5 *instructional skill*
Reading quickly and accurately	1 2 3 4 5 *reading skill*
Using words and punctuation correctly to express ideas well	1 2 3 4 5 *language usage skill*
Performing in sports activities	1 2 3 4 5 *athletic skill*

Abilities	Your Rating
Relating well to others	1 2 3 4 5 *social skill*
Selling products or services, motivating people to do something	1 2 3 4 5 *persuasion skill*
Using a library or laboratory to discover information and answers	1 2 3 4 5 *research skill*
Performing for others in drama, dance, comedy, and similar activities	1 2 3 4 5 *entertainment skill*
Typing, filing, copying, and other clerical work	1 2 3 4 5 *clerical skill*
Understanding and expressing ideas and relationships in words	1 2 3 4 5 *verbal skill*
Understanding and expressing ideas and relationships in numbers	1 2 3 4 5 *numerical skill*
Working with light, color, composition, and design to produce pictures or effects	1 2 3 4 5 *artistic skill*
Developing something new, ideas or things	1 2 3 4 5 *creative skill*
Repairing or working with machines, appliances, or tools	1 2 3 4 5 *mechanical skill*
Making things by hand—sewing, pottery making, carpentry, leatherwork, and the like	1 2 3 4 5 *craft skill*

WHAT DO YOU LIKE TO DO?

There are probably some tasks you are really good at and *don't* like to do—tasks that you excel at, but that bring you little or no satisfaction.

Everyday cleanup might come under that category. Most of us can do a pretty good job, but few of us really enjoy it. The next exercise asks that you consider tasks you really *like* to do.

This list is similar to the last one, but it has to do with INTERESTS. Check each item *high* or *low* according to how much you do or don't like to do it, or how much fun you think it is to do.

Low or 1 means: "I don't like doing it at all; definitely not my thing."

High or 5 means: "It's fun or most pleasurable." 4, 3, and 2 are degrees in between.

Rate yourself by circling the number that best indicates the amount of your INTEREST.

Interests	*Your Rating*
Singing, playing, or reading music	1 2 3 4 5 *musical interest*
Leading or supervising others	1 2 3 4 5 *supervisory skill*
Communicating ideas to others	1 2 3 4 5 *communication interest*
Visualizing shapes and surfaces from seeing drawings or plans	1 2 3 4 5 *spatial relations interest*
Thinking through complicated problems, carrying out logical processes in the mind	1 2 3 4 5 *abstract reasoning interest*
Bringing together things, information, and/or people to accomplish a task	1 2 3 4 5 *organizational interest*
Helping others make decisions and solve their problems	1 2 3 4 5 *counseling interest*
Teaching a skill or passing on knowledge to others	1 2 3 4 5 *instructional interest*
Reading quickly and accurately	1 2 3 4 5 *reading interest*
Using words and punctuation correctly to express ideas well	1 2 3 4 5 *language usage interest*

Interests	**Your Rating**
Performing in sports activities	1 2 3 4 5 *athletic interest*
Selling products or services, motivating people to do something	1 2 3 4 5 *persuasion interest*
Relating well to others	1 2 3 4 5 *social interest*
Using a library or laboratory to discover information and answers	1 2 3 4 5 *research interest*
Performing for others in drama, dance, comedy, and similar activities	1 2 3 4 5 *entertainment interest*
Typing, filing, copying, and other clerical work	1 2 3 4 5 *clerical interest*
Understanding and expressing ideas and relationships in words	1 2 3 4 5 *verbal interest*
Understanding and expressing ideas and relationships in numbers	1 2 3 4 5 *numerical interest*
Working with light, color, composition, and design to produce pictures or effects	1 2 3 4 5 *artistic interest*
Developing something new, things or ideas	1 2 3 4 5 *creative interest*
Repairing or working with machines, appliances, or tools	1 2 3 4 5 *mechanical interest*

Interests	*Your Rating*
Making things by hand—sewing, pottery making, carpentry, leatherwork, and the like	1 2 3 4 5 *craft interest*

Compile a list of your highest ABILITIES and INTERESTS by copying on the lists below every item to which you've given a rating of 4 or 5. Use the key words in parentheses below the number rating.

Your Abilities	*Your Interests*
_____	_____
_____	_____
_____	_____
_____	_____
_____	_____
_____	_____
_____	_____

Compare the lists. Which words or phrases appear on both? Write them in the SUMMARY CIRCLE below.

(SUMMARY CIRCLE)

_____ _____

_____ _____

_____

My Personality

CAN YOU FIND THE PATTERN?

Let's go back to the idea that we often let others tell us what we should do or like or what's fun and profitable. Giving in to other people's choices can bring us frustration. Their choices may not fit our personalities.

For example, if you are the type of person who enjoys reading books and talking with people and you read an article in the newspaper that says making your own clothes is the "in" thing to do, don't rush out and buy a sewing machine. Think about it. Do you really want to spend time concentrating on patterns and stitching and the like? Remember, that is time that you could spend reading or talking. If after thinking about it you still think it might be fun, then by all means go ahead. You may find a new, entertaining interest. But if it's really not for you, all the newspapers and all your friends are not going to keep you from becoming bored and dissatisfied with sewing.

What goes for hobbies, goes double for work. Satisfaction depends on whether the type of work you do complements your personality.

What kind of person are you?

What do you like to do?

What general categories fit you best when it comes to abilities and interests:

—social?
—realistic?
—enterprising?
—investigative?
—conventional?
—artistic?
—athletic?

Take a look at the chart on the following page. It describes seven different personality types in terms of what each type of person can do and likes to do. To rate your type, circle one of the numbers from 1 (for low) to 5 (for high) for your ability and for your interest. Then add the rating for ability to that for interest to get your total rating for each category.

I like talking to and being with people. I think that I would enjoy working with others and helping them with their problems. I enjoy doing things with my friends and making new friends. I would choose the kind of job that would let me attend meetings and work with other people.

My Ability Is: 1 2 3 4 5
My Interest Is: 1 2 3 4 5
              Social Total Score_____

I like to make things such as clothes, cabinets, pottery, jewelry, or machine parts. I am mechanically skillful and like to drive, operate, test, or repair things.

My Ability Is: 1 2 3 4 5
My Interest Is: 1 2 3 4 5
              Realistic Total Score_____

I enjoy competition and the rewards of leading others. I value the opportunity to influence other people and receive rewards, such as money or public recognition.

My Ability Is: 1 2 3 4 5
My Interest Is: 1 2 3 4 5
              Enterprising Total Score_____

I enjoy reading books and magazines about science or behavior (psychology, sociology). I find that I enjoy working in a lab or library on projects that allow me to find answers to unanswered questions. I enjoy solving number problems and games that make me think and concentrate.

My Ability Is: 1 2 3 4 5
My Interest Is: 1 2 3 4 5
Investigative Total Score_____

I am orderly and do tasks in a precise, accurate manner. I like to be organized, and I enjoy detail work. I deliberately plan to be productive in my work.

My Ability Is: 1 2 3 4 5
My Interest Is: 1 2 3 4 5
Conventional Total Score_____

I like to read and/or write stories. I enjoy listening to or playing in musical groups. I enjoy doing some of the following: photography, drawing, painting, and designing.

My Ability Is: 1 2 3 4 5
My Interest Is: 1 2 3 4 5
Artistic Total Score_____

I am very interested in my physical health and attractiveness. I like to be active in recreation and outdoor activities. Having good athletic skills is important to me.

My Ability Is: 1 2 3 4 5
My Interest Is: 1 2 3 4 5
Healthy-Athletic Total Score_____

When you have finished, list your top three categories below.

My Top Personality Traits

1. _____

2. _____

3. _____

There is still one more exercise to do before you can complete a well-rounded portrait of yourself, so read on.

A Job
to Enjoy

PUTTING YOUR WISHES INTO YOUR WORK

Obviously, not everyone can enjoy the one job or hobby he or she would love to do more than anything else. But all of us can think and dream about satisfying things we could be doing. (Or not doing! Gently swinging in a hammock can be lots of fun.)

Dreamers are everywhere.

There's the :

- traveling salesman who dreams of spending more time at home with his family;
- taxi driver who dreams of becoming a popular musician;
- single career woman who dreams of spending time with little children, or the mother who dreams of a satisfying career;
- truck driver who dreams of being a stockbroker;
- nurse who dreams of being a pilot, and
- college student who dreams of being a cowpoke.

Yes, we dream. We do that dreaming on the basis of our talents and strengths, plus the kinds of values that make up our lives. And out of that dreaming can come positive knowledge about ourselves and the kind of job we would feel good about.

Let's take an example to develop this idea. Suppose a man had the following top strengths and values:

Strengths	**Values**
persistent	endurance
curious	self-realization
goal-directed	achievement
precise	order
adventurous	variety

On the basis of these strengths and values, a counselor might suggest that he would be interested in such different types of jobs or hobbies as:

- running a retail store or shop
- being a policeman or investigator
- designing or drafting
- being a farmworker, conservationist, or gardener

Just as the man in the example, most of us have the potential for following many different interests. We may pursue them to earn money or simply as a hobby to pass the time more happily.

Of course, the chances of our actually doing one or the other are influenced by circumstances—the kind of education we got, the amount of time or money we have, obligations we may have to others, and so on. But our dreams reach through and beyond those limitations, and they, too, have a part in determining what we really do.

In the next exercise you will have a chance to cast off some of those limitations, give full reign to your dreams, and see what those dreams can tell you about finding a job you feel good about.

THE SHAPE OF A DREAM

First, let's think about the features that dream job would have—about the working conditions, the purpose of the job, your relations with other workers. What conditions would you choose? Look over the list on pages 84–85 and check off the features that are most important to you. Then imagine you have 1,000 points to divide up among the job features you have checked. You can divide up those points any way you want, according to how important each feature is to you.

For example, when one of the authors checked the list, she picked the following six features and then divided her 1,000 rating points as shown:

2. This job or hobby would require me to gain new information and develop judgment.

   I would rate 150 points

10. Through this job or hobby, I would have freedom to live my own way, to be the person I choose to be.

    I would rate 200 points

12. In this job or hobby, I would help other people.

    I would rate 200 points

14. This job or hobby would bring me into constant contact with someone I like or admire.

    I would rate 150 points

16. This job or hobby would demand my attention and continuing effort.

I would rate <u>100</u> points

17. In this job or hobby I would work with printed matter and/or numbers.

I would rate <u>200</u> points

_____

1,000 total

Now that you've seen how it's done, go ahead and do your own list. Pick as many or as few as you like, but remember: you only have 1,000 points to divide among your choices.

1. This job or hobby would require me to use my imagination in developing things or ideas.

I would rate ____ points

2. This job or hobby would allow me to gain new information and develop judgment.

I would rate ____ points

3. In this job or hobby, I would work closely with other people as a team.

I would rate ____ points

4. I would be in no danger of losing this job or hobby.

I would rate ____ points

5. This job or hobby would bring me admiration from my friends and fellow workers.

I would rate ____ points

6. In this job or hobby, I could be neat and clean, and my duties would not vary.

I would rate ____ points

7. This job or hobby would bring me opportunity to influence others.

I would rate ____ points

8. In this job or hobby, I would be my own boss.

I would rate ____ points

9. Through this job or hobby, I could help make the world beautiful.

I would rate ____ points

10. Through this job or hobby, I would have freedom to live my own way, be the person I choose to be.

I would rate ____ points

11. This job or hobby would take a lot of my time and talent to do well.

I would rate ____ points

12. In this job or hobby, I would help other people.

I would rate ____ points

13. This job or hobby would bring in lots of money for me.

I would rate ____ points

14. This job or hobby would bring me into constant contact with someone I like or admire.

I would rate ____ points

15. This job or hobby would offer me different kinds of tasks.

I would rate ____ points

16. This job or hobby would demand my attention and continuing efforts.

I would rate ____ points

17. In this job or hobby, I would work with printed materials and/or numbers.

I would rate ____ points

18. In this job or hobby, I work directly with people and have the chance to know them well.

I would rate ____ points

19. In this job or hobby, using my hands and tools would be the most important feature.

I would rate ____ points

Have you finished checking the features you would want in your dream job and divided up the 1,000 points between them? All right, now circle the five features to which you have awarded the highest number of points.

As you were doing the chart, you probably noticed that each feature is numbered. Each feature corresponds to a Career Value just as your rewards on the Good Times Chart did. The numbers and values below show you which Career Value each feature is related to.

1—creativity	11—achievement
2—knowledge	12—social service
3—relating	13—economic reward
4—security	14—cooperation
5—prestige	15—variety
6—order	16—endurance
7—leadership	17—data
8—independence	18—people
9—beauty	19—things
10—self-realization	

Using this key, find the career values that your five top dream job features correspond to and record them below.

FIVE TOP CAREER VALUES FROM THE DREAM JOB

_____

_____

_____

_____

_____

Refer back to page 39 to find your top values from the Good Times Chart and write them in the spaces below.

FIVE TOP CAREER VALUES FROM THE GOOD TIMES CHART

_____

_____

_____

_____

_____

If any values appear on both lists, write them in this next set of spaces. Fill in the remaining spaces with the values you think are the most important still left on either list.

MOST IMPORTANT CAREER VALUES

_____

_____

_____

_____

_____

What you have done should have revealed what is important to you from a couple of different directions. This way, you get a better reading on the kinds of jobs you would really feel good about. Now you are ready to put it all together into that big picture of you.

The Full Picture

PUTTING IT ALL TOGETHER

Each of the exercises done so far has been in preparation for your Full Picture Chart. Now you are ready to put it all together.

The idea is to fill in the chart with what you have learned in the various exercises and then judge two past experiences—one good and one bad—on the basis of that new self-knowledge.

First let's fill in the Full Picture Chart with information from the exercises you have done. Refer to page 49 to see what your Strength Categories are. Then write them down in the spaces provided in the left-hand column of the chart. Do the same with Data, People, Things (from page 59), your Abilities and Interests (from page 69), your Career Values (from page 87), and finally your Top Personality Traits (from page 76).

As you are filling in the chart, think about each item and what it tells you about yourself, about the kind of person you are.

Now that you have filled in the whole left-hand column, let's see how that self-portrait relates to some of your actual experiences. Everyone has had some pleasant work experiences and, sadly enough, some unpleasant ones. And they may be quite different things for different people. A racing-car driver may enjoy the danger and excitement of the race while another person would simply be terrified. Someone else might feel best with the order, routine, and security of an office job, while a friend thinks it is deadly boring. A forest ranger who likes the quiet and solitude of his job might be driven insane by the shouting, competition, and frenzy of the grain-trading pits.

Think back over the past few years and pick out two experiences from work or school—one that was very pleasant and rewarding and another that was very unpleasant, frustrating, or irritating. One could be a class or teacher at school that you particularly enjoyed or a job that seemed "just right"—something you were glad to go to each morning. The other should be just the opposite, a class you dreaded going to or a job you hated the thought of.

Take a word or two that identifies the happy experience and write them in the space over the happy face on the chart. Then do the same with the unhappy experience over the sad face on the chart.

Your next move is to see how your happy and sad experiences match with your strengths, values, interests, and the rest. Look at your first Strength Value. Did your happy experience come partly because of that strength? Did the experience help to reinforce that strength? If you feel there is a strong positive connection between the experience and the strength, place a "5" in the box where the happy experience column meets the strength line.

My Full Picture Chart

Strength Categories	
Data People Things	
Abilities Interests	
Career Values	
Personality Traits	

Totals

☺	☹	A	B	C	D	E

If the connection is positive but not quite so strong, mark a "4." For a so-so connection between them mark "3," and for a weak or negative connection mark "2." Finally, if there seems to be no connection or the strength and experience seem to be at odds with each other, mark a "1."

Let's take an example to show just how to evaluate it. Perhaps two of your Strength Categories were security and independence, and your happy experience was with a pleasant office job that had a regular routine and few surprises. You might rate it 5 on security but decide that it did not give you much independence; so you might give it only 2 on that Strength Value.

Go through the whole list for your happy experience, then go back and rate your sad experience. That way you'll be concentrating on one experience at a time and can develop a better "feel" for how it matches or conflicts with your various values and qualities.

Got them all done? Then it's time to total up the scores for your happy and sad experiences. Your happy experience probably received a higher score because it matched your values and characteristics much more closely. Now you can begin to see that there is a real connection between the kind of person you are and the kind of job you feel good about.

Looking into the Future

Here's where you get to do some of the things you've gone through all the exercises for. You can use the knowledge from your Full Picture Chart to pick future jobs that fit you—your standards and values, your strengths, abilities, and interests.

Okay, here goes. At the top of columns A and B on your chart, write in two jobs or kinds of work that you think you would like to do. At the top of columns C and D, write in two kinds of volunteer work, hobbies, or recreational activities that you like to spend time with. Finally, at the top of column E, write in a fantasy job, hobby, or activity that you think would be very satisfying. (This can be something new; you don't have to use the same imaginary job you listed on your Good Times Chart, but again assume you have all the time and ability you need to do whatever you choose.)

Now rate the jobs and activities in columns A through E the same way you did your happy and sad experiences. If you have chosen wisely, your scores should run closer to your happy experience than to your sad one. But whatever the score, the pattern for each job or activity should give a good idea of why you chose it and how it really would fit you.

Look over the scores. Were there some surprises? What did you discover about yourself and your world? Now it's time to put that knowledge to *work*.

Doing It

WHAT NOW?

You probably started this book because you felt the need for some guidance in planning for your future. You were dissatisfied with your present situation or a bit unsure of just where you should go in life.

At this point you know a good deal more about yourself and what makes you comfortable, but you may be wondering just how to relate that to career planning and job hunting.

When it comes to change, some people can take off in another direction very easily. They don't need to look back. They don't have time to regret things left behind.

Others are made differently. They either feel no need for personal change, or their living situation just doesn't make change possible. Life seems to have them boxed in.

The way out, the way to change, the way to make life and work more satisfying, is through small, simple, seemingly insignificant beginnings.

Make some small openings in your life!

EASE into change.

DO IT. Take up a new hobby or recreation in its least expensive and least time-consuming form. If your changes have to be a secret at first, do it that way.

BE AN OBSERVER. Take any opportunity to watch somebody else doing the activity.

MEET PEOPLE INVOLVED. Talking to them may eventually get you involved as well.

VOLUNTEER to help. This is one of the best ways of getting into something you've always wanted to do.

One day you may find that those small changes have led to larger, more satisfying changes.

Via your Full Picture Chart, you now have a good idea about your values for a career and life-style:

- the conditions you need in a job as well as
- the living conditions that round out a good existence.

Now the question comes: "How do I find out about the kinds of work that correlate with my value needs?"

Use the chart two ways!

1. Look for broad work categories that require similar skills (your specific skills).
2. Pinpoint the work market into which your specific skills fit.

99

Let's take number 1. Look for broad career categories on your Full Picture Chart.

Each job uses skills that actually fit more than one occupation.

Skill with DATA fits the

—mailman
—pollster
—librarian
—architect
—file clerk
—treasurer.

Perhaps none of these examples fit you, but you're still primarily a Data person.

So the rest of your chart is very important. It gives clues about specific jobs where you will fit. The idea is to discover *patterns* or broad categories. Counselor Kathy Sims* uses a method called "synthesization," or revealing the wide career categories found on your own chart. In the following example, Sims explains how one student's strengths in both music and counseling led her into music therapy as a career. Then Sims demonstrates how the synthesized chart helped pinpoint a definite and satisfying career for this student.

*Union Free School District, East Aurora, New York.

Here is how the information on the student's Full Picture Chart was used to produce some answers:

STRENGTH CATEGORIES
Independent
Thoughtful
Open-minded
Musical
Growing

DATA–PEOPLE–THINGS
Counseling
Teaching
Performing

ABILITIES/INTERESTS
Musical
Counseling
Instructional
Social

CAREER VALUES
Relating
Beauty
Variety
Independence
Social Service

PERSONALITY TRAITS
Social
Artistic
Investigative

Sims noted that counseling, teaching, social service, and relating to people were allied activities that showed up repeatedly on the chart along with the strong combination of musical, artistic, and performing interests. Finally, there was a marked tendency to independence and variety.

This girl did well in languages and music. However, she had no interest in a music career and felt that language careers were far too competitive and scarce. She began looking at counseling, specifically music therapy, in which strong linguistic skill would also be useful. Music therapy would demand the use of all of her skills and fill her personality needs, including the need for independence and a variety of duties.

Try the same technique on your chart.

Several broad categories were found on the student's chart:

- music
- instructing
- counseling
- social service

Another person might discover the same broad categories and yet end up in a totally different job or career.

Each of us is built for a different career and for a different level of any career.

Our levels of *ability and education* make the difference. For example, the person with interest in teaching has these options:

EDUCATION	POSSIBLE CAREER
Elementary or high school	Teacher aide
Undergraduate degree	Teacher, elementary or high school
Post-graduate degree	Teaching instructor, department head or administrator

As levels of ability and education increase, careers can become more complex. We see this illustrated by the construction industry. The complexity might run:

- bricklayer, carpenter
- construction engineer
- architect
- officer, engineering company
- officer, construction company

So any given career category requires people of many levels of skill.

Having seen general patterns or career categories, you may now *determine the work market* into which your skills fit.

The first task is to match up your career values with specific job skills listed on the next page. There are sixteen different skills possible within your Full Picture Chart.

SIXTEEN JOB SKILLS THAT RELATE TO FULL PICTURE CHART CAREER VALUES

1. Work with things; generally requires manual skills.
2. Work with ideas; use intellect to solve problems or to create.
3. Help people; serve or assist others in accomplishing a task or goal.
4. Work with people; in company of others; need for an amiable personality.
5. See physical results; work produces tangible product.

6. Opportunity for self-expression; freedom to use own ideas.
7. Work as part of a team; cooperate to reach a goal.
8. Work independently; be self-motivated.
9. Work closely supervised; performance and standards controlled by supervisor.
10. Direct activities of others; supervisory responsibility.
11. High level of responsibility; involves decision about finance and human welfare.
12. Physical stamina for continual lifting, standing, running, walking.
13. Work with detail; process technical data or written material daily.
14. Repetitious work; perform same task daily.
15. Motivate or influence others to produce.
16. Competitive; achieve by competing with others for recognition and advancement.

Which of these job skills characterizes you? Your Full Picture Chart matched to the items shown should clearly define your job skills.

To match your personal characteristics with activities related to specific types of jobs, match up the items on your Full Picture Chart with the list of job characteristics as shown on the Job Skill Chart on page 106–107. Go through it section by section and check off each listing that corresponds to what you have on your Full Picture Chart.

Job Skill Chart

FULL PICTURE CHART CATEGORIES

JOB CHARACTERISTICS	ABILITIES/INTERESTS
1. Work with things; generally requires manual skills.	spatial relations, artistic, mechanical, craft
2. Work with ideas; use intellect to solve problems or to create.	abstract reasoning, language usage, research, verbal, numerical, creative
3. Help people; serve or assist others in accomplishing a task or goal.	supervisory, counseling, instructional, social
4. Work with people; in company of others; need for an amiable personality.	communication, organizational, counseling, instructional, persuasion, social, entertainment
5. See physical results; work produces tangible product.	abstract reasoning, clerical, artistic, mechanical, craft
6. Opportunity for self-expression; freedom to use own ideas.	musical, communication, entertainment, verbal, artistic, creative, craft
7. Work as part of a team; cooperate to reach a goal.	communication, instructional, athletic, social, clerical
8. Work independently; be self-motivated.	musical, abstract reasoning, reading, language usage, athletic, research, clerical, artistic, creative, mechanical, craft
9. Work closely supervised; performance and standards controlled by supervisor.	musical, athletic, persuasion, entertainment, clerical, mechanical, craft
10. Direct activities of others; supervisory responsibility.	musical, supervisory, organizational, verbal, instructional, numerical, mechanical
11. High level of responsibility; involves decision about finance and human welfare.	musical, supervisory, communication, organizational, reading, verbal
12. Physical stamina for continual lifting, standing, running, walking.	athletic, entertainment, mechanical
13. Work with detail; process technical data or written material daily.	communication, spatial relations, organizational, instructional, reading, language usage, clerical, verbal, numerical
14. Repetitious work; perform same task daily.	musical, communication, instructional, language usage, persuasion, verbal, numerical
15. Motivate or influence others to produce.	supervisory, instructional, persuasion
16. Competitive; achieve by competing with others for recognition and advancement.	supervisory, athletic, entertainment

DATA, PEOPLE, THINGS	CAREER VALUES	PERSONALITY TRAITS
Items from the THINGS category	self-realization, things	realistic, artistic
Items from the DATA category	creativity, knowledge, self-realization, data	enterprising, investigative
Items from the PEOPLE category	relating, self-realization, social service, people	social, enterprising
Items from the PEOPLE category	relating, self-realization, social service, people	social, enterprising
Items from the DATA and THINGS category	beauty, self-realization, people	realistic, artistic, conventional
Items from the PEOPLE category	creativity, knowledge, independence, beauty, achievement, variety	enterprising, investigative, artistic
Items from the PEOPLE category	relating, security, cooperation, variety	social, enterprising, healthy-athletic
Items from all categories	creativity, knowledge, order, independence, achievement, variety	realistic, conventional, enterprising, artistic, investigative
Items from all categories	relating, security, order, economic reward, cooperation	conventional
Items from all categories	leadership, achievement, social service, economic reward, endurance	social, enterprising
Items from all categories	knowledge, prestige, self-realization, achievement, social service, econ. reward	social, enterprising
Items from the THINGS category	self-realization, endurance, things	enterprising
Items from the DATA and THINGS categories	knowledge, self-realization, endurance, data, things	investigative, conventional
Items from all categories	security, order, social service	realistic, conventional
Items from the PEOPLE category	leadership, beauty, people, achievement, social service	social, artistic, enterprising
Items from the PEOPLE category	prestige, achievement, economic reward, people	enterprising

As you complete your check of each section, a pattern will begin to appear. Write down each of the job characteristics that match one or more of your Full Picture Chart characteristics. For example, if you had "organizational" under Interest/Abilities on your Full Picture Chart, you would list 4, 10, 11, and 13 from the job characteristics. Similarly, if you had "cooperation" under Career Values, you would list 7 and 9 from the job characteristics. Do *not* list those characteristics that have only been checked because they correspond to "all categories" under Data, People, Things.

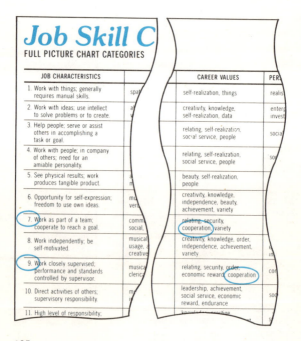

Job Skill C
FULL PICTURE CHART CATEGORIES

JOB CHARACTERISTICS		CAREER VALUES	PER
1. Work with things; generally requires manual skills.	spa	self-realization, things	realis
2. Work with ideas; use intellect to solve problems or to create.	a	creativity, knowledge, self-realization, data	enter invest
3. Help people; serve or assist others in accomplishing a task or goal.		relating, self-realization, social service, people	socia
4. Work with people; in company of others; need for an amiable personality.		relating, self-realization, social service, people	so
5. See physical results; work produces tangible product.	a m	beauty, self-realization, people	
6. Opportunity for self-expression; freedom to use own ideas.	mu ver	creativity, knowledge, independence, beauty, achievement, variety	
7. Work as part of a team; Cooperate to reach a goal.	comm social,	relating, security, cooperation, variety	
8. Work independently; be self-motivated.	musical usage, a creative	creativity, knowledge, order, independence, achievement, variety	in
9. Work closely supervised; performance and standards controlled by supervisor.	musica cleric	relating, security, order, economic reward cooperation	co
10. Direct activities of others; supervisory responsibility.	m	leadership, achievement, social service, economic reward, endurance	so
11. High level of responsibility;			

FROM SKILLS TO OCCUPATIONS

The last chart—on the next pages—matches those job characteristics to a sampling of specific occupations. Note the job characteristics you have listed and see where they correspond to the various occupations listed. By marking your job characteristics and following the column down through the various characteristics, you can determine the types of occupations that would best suit you. Remember that the occupations listed are just a suggestive sampling. There are many, many more similar jobs that would also be of interest for you.

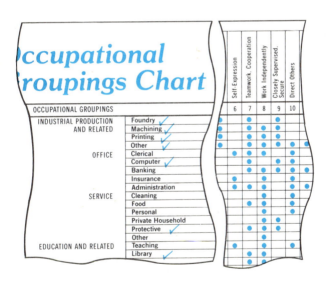

Occupational Groupings Chart

OCCUPATIONAL GROUPINGS		Self-Expression	Teamwork, Cooperation	Work Independently	Closely Supervised, Secure	Direct Others
		6	7	8	9	10
INDUSTRIAL PRODUCTION AND RELATED	Foundry		•		•	
	Machining		•	•	•	
	Printing		•	•	•	
	Other		•	•	•	•
OFFICE	Clerical	•	•	•		•
	Computer		•		•	•
	Banking		•	•	•	•
	Insurance	•		•		•
	Administration	•	•	•		•
SERVICE	Cleaning			•		•
	Food		•	•		•
	Personal			•		•
	Private Household			•	•	
	Protective		•	•	•	
	Other			•		
EDUCATION AND RELATED	Teaching	•		•		•
	Library		•	•		

109

Occupational Groupings Chart

OCCUPATIONAL GROUPINGS	
INDUSTRIAL PRODUCTION AND RELATED	Foundry
	Machining
	Printing
	Other
OFFICE	Clerical
	Computer
	Banking
	Insurance
	Administration
SERVICE	Cleaning
	Food
	Personal
	Private Household
	Protective
	Other
EDUCATION AND RELATED	Teaching
	Library
SALES	
CONSTRUCTION	
TRANSPORTATION	Aviation
	Merchant Marine
	Railroading
	Driving
SCIENTIFIC AND TECHNICAL	Conservation
	Engineering
	Technical
MECHANICAL AND REPAIR	Telephone Craft
	Other
HEALTH CARE	Dental
	Medical Practice
	Medical Technical Assistance
	Nursing
	Therapy and Rehabilitation
	Other
SOCIAL SCIENCE	
SOCIAL SERVICE	Counseling
	Religious Vocation
	Other
ART, DESIGN, COMMUNICATION	Performing Arts
	Design
	Communications

Manual Skills	Use Intellect	Help People, Serve, Assist	Work with People	See Physical Results	Self-Expression	Teamwork, Cooperation	Work Independently	Closely Supervised, Secure	Direct Others	Responsibility	Physical Stamina	Detail Work	Repetitive Work	Motivate Others	Competitive
1	2	3	4	5	6	7	8	9	10	11	12	13	14	15	16
●				●		●		●				●			
●				●		●	●	●			●	●	●		
●				●		●	●	●				●	●		
●			●	●		●	●	●	●	●	●		●		
●	●	●			●	●	●		●			●	●		
●	●						●		●	●		●	●		
	●	●				●		●	●	●		●	●		
	●	●	●		●		●		●			●	●		
	●	●	●		●	●		●	●	●		●	●	●	
●		●						●	●		●	●			
●		●	●			●		●	●		●		●		
		●	●	●				●	●		●		●		
●							●	●							
●	●		●			●		●		●	●	●	●		
●		●						●			●				
	●	●	●		●			●	●	●			●	●	
	●					●	●					●			
●	●	●	●			●	●	●	●	●	●	●	●	●	●
●			●			●	●	●	●	●	●		●		
●	●	●	●			●			●	●	●	●			
●	●					●			●	●	●	●			
●		●	●			●	●	●	●	●	●	●	●		
●		●					●				●				●
●	●					●	●		●	●	●	●			
	●			●	●	●			●	●	●	●			
●	●		●			●	●		●			●			
●			●			●	●	●			●	●	●		
		●	●	●	●	●	●	●				●	●		
		●	●	●	●		●				●	●			
●	●	●	●			●	●	●	●	●		●	●		
		●	●				●			●					
		●	●	●	●	●	●	●	●	●		●			
●	●	●	●				●		●	●		●			
	●				●		●					●			
		●	●	●		●	●		●	●				●	
		●	●					●						●	
	●	●	●		●		●		●	●	●	●		●	
	●			●	●										●
●		●			●	●	●	●	●	●		●		●	●
	●	●	●	●	●	●	●			●	●	●		●	●

These are the large occupational groupings into which you can most comfortably fit. Your skills are highly useful somewhere within these careers. For immediate, clear, and concise information, see the *Occupational Outlook Handbook* published each year by the U.S. Government Printing Office. Also very helpful are the *College Graduate's Occupational Outlook* and *Occupational Manpower and Training Needs,* both compiled by the U.S. Department of Labor.

All of this can help you get started in the right direction. But the next move is yours!

Good Luck!